THE AUDUBON NOTEBOOK

An Illustrated Journal with space for notes

Beauty is nature's coin.
—JOHN MILTON

Pine Warbler

The greater the efforts we make to fathom the secrets of the birds, the more our knowledge expands, the clearer becomes our realization that the secrets of the birds will remain mysteries of nature as long as she abounds with the miracles of life.

—HANS DOSSENBACH

Snowy Owl

Commonly we stride through the out-of-doors too swiftly to see more than the most obvious and prominent things. For observing nature, the best pace is a snail's pace.

—EDWIN WAY TEALE

Band-tailed Pigeon

In nature there are neither rewards nor punishments—only consequences.
                                        —ROBERT G. INGERSOLL

Caracara

I go to Nature to be soothed and healed, and to have my senses put in tune once more.

—JOHN BURROUGHS

Fork-tailed Flycatcher

It is always sunrise somewhere; the dew is never all dried at once;
a shower is forever falling; vapor is forever rising.

—JOHN MUIR

Trumpeter Swan

To be a bird is to be alive more intensively than any other living creature
. . . (Birds) live in a world that is always the present, mostly full of joy.

—N.J. BERRILL

Black-throated Mango

You must not know too much, or be too precise or scientific about birds and trees and flowers. A certain free margin . . . helps your enjoyment of these things.

—WALT WHITMAN

Great Blue Heron

The songs of the birds were so pleasant that it seemed as if a man could never wish to leave the place. The flocks of parrots concealed the sun; and the birds were so numerous, and of so many different kinds, that it was wonderful.

—CHRISTOPHER COLUMBUS

American Magpie

I never for a day gave up listening to the songs of our birds, or watching their peculiar habits, or delineating them in the best way that I could.

—JOHN JAMES AUDUBON

Yellow-throated Vireo

Nature is visible thought.
—HEINRICH HEINE

Brown Pelican

One touch of nature makes the whole world kin.
—WILLIAM SHAKESPEARE

Carolina Parakeet

Nature is trying very hard to make us succeed, but nature does not depend on us. We are not the only experiment.

—RICHARD BUCKMINISTER FULLER

Barrow's Goldeneye

Nature is always hinting at us. It hints over and over again.
And suddenly we take the hint.

—ROBERT FROST

Great Gray Owl

Nothing wholly admirable ever happened in this country except the migration of birds.

—BROOKS ATKINSON

Chickadees and Bushtit

I never saw a wild thing sorry for itself.
—D.H. LAWRENCE

Great Black-backed Gull

The field has eyes, the wood has ears; I will look, be silent, and listen.
—HIERONYMUS BOSCH

Yellow-breasted Chat

Nature always has the last word.
—JOHN STEWART COLLIS

Louisiana Heron

*Nature is not a competition. it doesn't really matter, when you go out,
if you don't identify anything. What matters is the feeling heart.*

—RICHARD ADAMS

Buff-breasted Sandpiper

Nature does not care whether the hunter slays the beast or the beast the hunter. She will make good compost of them both, and her ends are prospered whichever succeeds.

—JOHN BURROUGHS

California Condor

Every human being looks to the birds. They suit the fancy of us all. What they feel they can voice, as we try to; they court and nest, they battle with the elements, they are torn by two opposing impulses, a love of home and a passion for far places. Only with birds do we share so much emotion.

—DONALD CULROSS PEATTIE

Barn Swallow

Sweet is the breath of morn, her rising sweet with charm of earliest birds.
—JOHN MILTON

Say's Phoebe, Western Kingbird, Scissor-tailed Flycatcher

In a world that seems so very puzzling is it any wonder birds have such appeal? Birds are, perhaps, the most eloquent expression of reality.

—ROGER TORY PETERSON

Gyrfalcon

I know of no sculpture, painting or music that exceeds the compelling spiritual command of the soaring shape of granite cliff and dome, of patina of light on rock and forest, and of the thunder and whispering of the falling, flowing waters.

—ANSEL ADAMS

Long-tailed Jaeger

Nature provides exceptions to every rule.
—MARGARET FULLER

House Wren

The wild goose comes north with the voice of freedom and adventure. He is more than a big, far-ranging bird, he is the epitome of wanderlust, limitless horizons, and distant travel. He is the yearning and the dream, the search and the wonder, the unfettered foot and the wind's-will wing.

—HAL BORLAND

Canada Goose

Never does nature say one thing and wisdom another.
—JUVENAL

Great Horned Owl

Nature never blunders; when she makes a fool she means it.
—JOSH BILLINGS

Purple Gallinule

Nature's laws affirm instead of prohibiting. If you violate her laws you are your own prosecuting attorney, judge, jury, and hangman.

—LUTHER BURBANK

Osprey

Nature does nothing uselessly.
—ARISTOTLE

Snowy Heron

Although birds coexist with us on this eroded planet, they live independently of us with a self-sufficiency that is almost a rebuke. In the world of birds a symposium on the purpose of life would be inconceivable. They do not need it. We are not that self reliant. We are the ones who have lost our way.

—BROOKS ATKINSON

Great Crested Grebe

Nature is what she is—amoral and persistent.
—STEPHEN JAY GOULD

Common Grackle

Forget not that the earth delights to feel your bare feet
and the winds long to play with your hair.

—KAHLIL GIBRAN

Sandhill Crane

Without birds, where would we have learned that there can be song in the heart?

—HAL BORLAND

Yellowthroat

There are homilies in nature's work worth all the wisdom
of the schools, if we could but read them rightly.

—WASHINGTON IRVING

Red-throated Loon

Nature, in her blind search for life, has filled every possible cranny of the earth with some sort of fantastic creature.

—JOSEPH WOOD KRUTCH

White Pelican

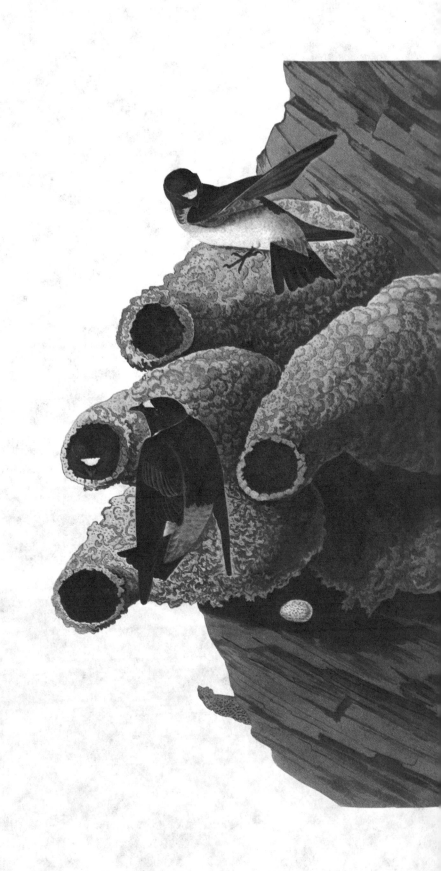

Civilization no longer needs to open up wilderness; it needs wilderness to help open up the still largely unexplored human mind.

—DAVID RAINS WALLACE

Cliff Swallow

All nature wears one universal grin.
—HENRY FIELDING

Horned Puffin

Nature thrives on patience.
—PAUL BOESE

Red-headed Woodpecker

Man must understand his universe in order to understand his destiny.

—NEIL ARMSTRONG

Bald Eagle

I do not know of a single flowering plant that tastes good and is poisonous. Nature is not out to get us.

—EUELL GIBBONS

Hooded Warbler

Nothing which we can imagine about Nature is incredible.
—PLINY THE ELDER

Magnificent Frigatebird

Nature is not benevolent; Nature is just, gives pound for pound, measure for measure, makes no exceptions, never tempers her decrees with mercy, or winks at any infringement of her laws.

—JOHN BURROUGHS

Red-eyed Vireo

Like a great poet, Nature knows how to produce the greatest effects with the most limited means.

—HEINRICH HEINE

Spruce Grouse

There are no wild animals till man makes them so.
                                    —MARK TWAIN

Wild Turkey

The beauty and genius of a work of art may be reconceived, though its first material expression be destroyed; a vanished harmony may yet again inspire the composer; but when the last individual of a race of living things breathes no more, another heaven and another earth must pass before such a one can be again.

—WILLIAM BEEBE

Passenger Pigeon

There are no grostesques in nature.
—THOMAS BROWNE

Anhinga